Pet Toxic Foods & Hazards Quick Reference Guide

CONTENTS

Use the page numbers to locate risks at home and outdoors. When in doubt, call your vet.

CALL YOUR VET FIRST

Don't wait, time is critical. Always phone your vet or a 24/7 emergency veterinary hospital if you suspect poisoning.

DON'T INDUCE VOMITING

Unless a vet specifically tells you, never try to make your pet vomit. Some toxins cause more harm coming back up.

CHECK & SAVE THE PACKAGING

Bring labels, wrappers, or plant samples to the vet. It helps them act faster.

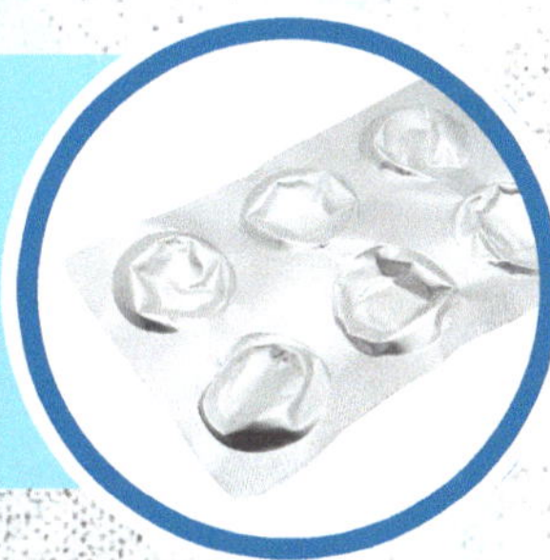

LEARN THE EARLY SIGNS

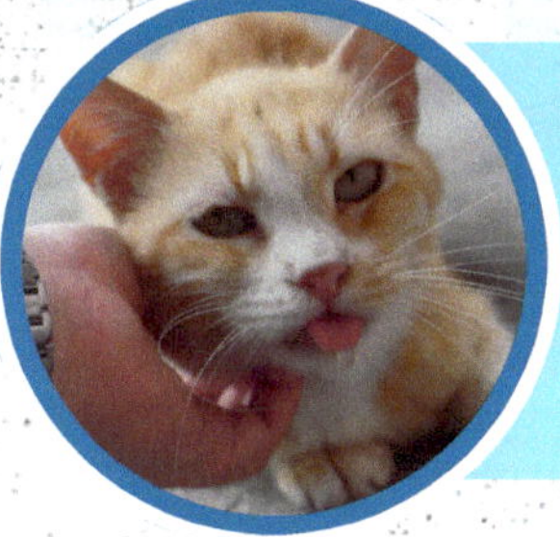

Watch for drooling, vomiting, tremors, or unusual behavior. Acting quickly when symptoms first appear can save your pet's life.

When in doubt, call your vet first.

CHOCOLATE & COCOA

Sweet for us, toxic for them.
Theobromine and caffeine
overstimulate the heart and nervous
system. Even a small bite can cause
real harm.

GRAPES & RAISINS

Even a few grapes or raisins can
cause sudden kidney failure in dogs.
Cats rarely eat them, but keep all
dried fruit out of reach.

ONION & GARLIC

Fresh, cooked, or powdered, all
forms damage red blood cells. This
can lead to anemia, weakness, and
costly vet treatment.

XYLITOL

Found in sugar-free gum, candy, some
peanut butters, and toothpaste. This
artificial sweetener causes a rapid
drop in blood sugar and can destroy
the liver in dogs.

**Even a small snack can cause
a big problem.**

TOXIC FOODS

PART 2

Kitchen staples and condiments
that are unsafe for pets.

ALCOHOL & RAW DOUGH

Fermenting dough produces alcohol and gas. This can lead to dangerous bloating, intoxication, and even respiratory distress in pets.

CAFFEINE

Coffee, tea, and energy drinks can cause restlessness, tremors, and abnormal heart rhythms. Caffeine is unsafe for both dogs and cats.

MACADAMIA NUTS

Uniquely toxic to dogs, even a handful can cause weakness, tremors, and joint pain. Cats aren't affected, but never give nuts to pets.

CANNABIS EDIBLES (THC)

Cookies, brownies, gummies. Can cause agitation, wobbling, dribbling urine, and collapse. Chocolate or xylitol may make it more dangerous.

The safest treat is one made for pets.

AVOCADO (FLESH, PIT, SKIN)

Contains persin and lots of fat. Ingestion can cause vomiting and pancreatitis. Keep guac and pits away from pets.

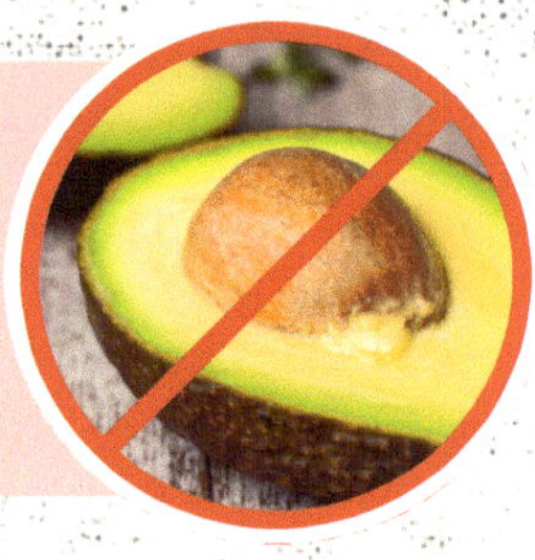

POTATO SPROUTS & GREEN PEELS

Green parts and sprouts are toxic. Eating them can cause vomiting and weakness. Discard green or sprouted potatoes.

HOPS (HOME BREWING)

Hops can trigger dangerous overheating in dogs. Signs include agitation and rapid breathing. Keep brew waste well secured.

SALT & BRINES

High sodium is hazardous. Gulping brine can cause vomiting and seizures. Rinse spills and offer fresh water.

Skip table scraps and choose pet-safe treats.

THYROID MEDS (LEVOTHYROXINE)

Human doses are far too strong. Overdose can cause agitation and fast heart rate. Keep bottles closed and out of reach.

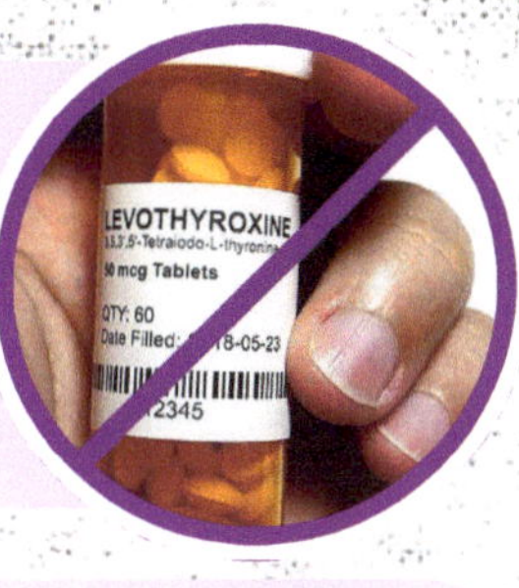

OPIOID PAIN MEDS

Opioids depress breathing and alertness. Pets may drool, wobble, or collapse. Treat as an emergency and call your vet.

5-FLUOROURACIL (5-FU) CREAMS

Tiny amounts are highly toxic if licked. Signs include vomiting, seizures, and collapse. Store securely and wash hands after use.

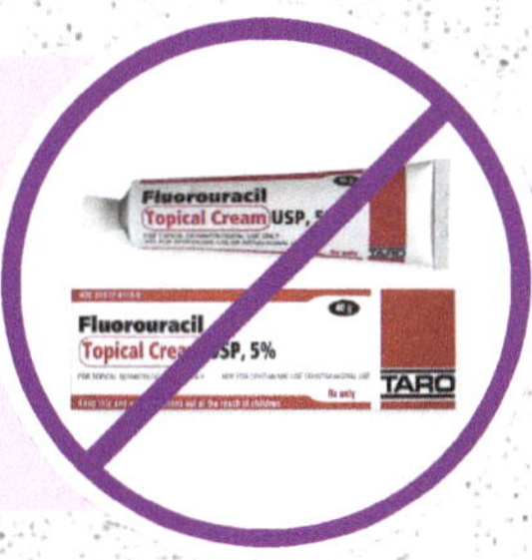

TOPICAL ANESTHETICS

Gels and sprays can be dangerous if swallowed. Exposure may cause vomiting and tremors. Prevent licking and keep products away.

Lock meds away and ask your vet first.

indoor & outdoor PLANTS

PART 1

Common indoor & outdoor plants that can harm pets.

LILIES

Extremely toxic to cats, even pollen or vase water can cause kidney failure that is often fatal. Dogs are not usually affected but should still be kept away.

SAGO PALM/CYCADS

Seeds are the most toxic part. Ingestion can cause vomiting, seizures, and severe liver damage.

OLEANDER (NERIUM)

Highly poisonous if chewed. Even small amounts can disrupt heart rhythm and be life-threatening.

BRUNFELSIA (YESTERDAY-TODAY-TOMORROW)

Often grown in gardens. Causes drooling, tremors, and seizures in dogs; cats have also been affected in rare cases.

If you're unsure, keep paws away from plants.

hazardous PLANTS

PART 2

Ornamentals and bouquets
that are known to be toxic.

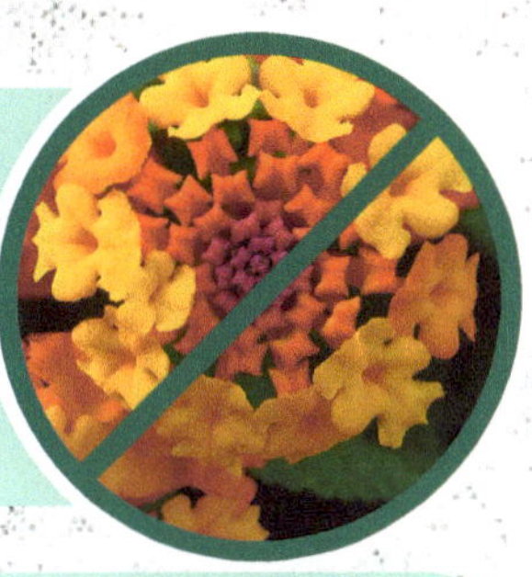

LANTANA

Common in backyards. Can cause
vomiting, weakness, and liver
damage.

PHILODENDRON/POTHOS

Contain crystals that irritate the
mouth, tongue, and throat. Pets can
drool and struggle to swallow.

AZALEAS

Vibrant flowers but highly toxic.
Can cause drooling, vomiting,
and dangerous heart issues.

OTHER TOXIC VARIETIES

Many common ornamentals pose
risks. Always check before planting or
bringing new greenery home.

**Check before you plant.
Prevention saves lives.**

DIEFFENBACHIA (DUMB CANE)
Chewing releases needle-like crystals.
Pets drool, paw at the mouth, and
swell. Keep all stems and leaves away.

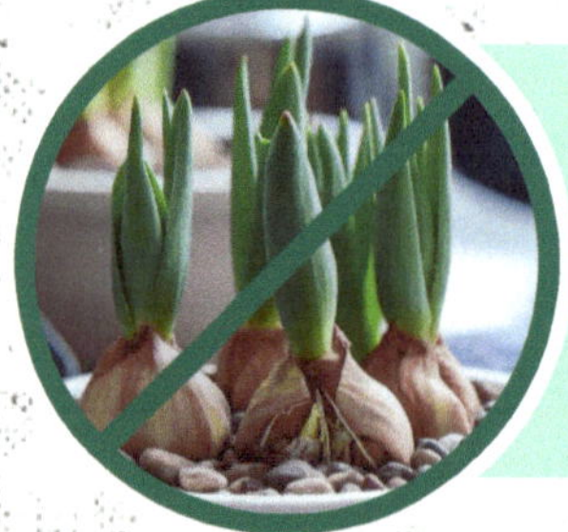

TULIPS & DAFFODILS (BULBS)
Bulbs are the most toxic part. Ingestion
can cause vomiting and lethargy. Don't
let pets dig or chew stored bulbs.

YEW (TAXUS SPECIES)
All parts contain potent heart toxins.
Even small amounts can be fatal.
Keep clippings and berries off lawns.

AUTUMN CROCUS (COLCHICUM)
Highly toxic plant. Causes severe
vomiting and organ damage. Seek
urgent vet care after any ingestion.

**When unsure, choose
pet-safe varieties.**

COCOA SHELL MULCH

Mulch smells like chocolate and tempts dogs. Theobromine can cause heart and nerve signs. Choose pet-safe mulch instead.

FERTILIZER SPIKES & GRANULES

Chewing can trigger GI upset and pancreatitis. Oils and salts add risk. Store securely and apply exactly as directed.

COMPOST TEA CONCENTRATES

Bacteria and molds can make pets sick. Ingestion may cause vomiting and diarrhea. Keep containers sealed and rinse equipment.

HOSE & POOL CHEMICALS

Chlorine and algaecides can burn mouths and throats. Drinking solutions is dangerous. Store high and mix away from pets.

Store safely and keep pets off treated areas.

HOUSEHOLD
PART 1

Common home products
that can poison pets.

ESSENTIAL OILS

Tea tree, eucalyptus, and many others
are especially toxic to cats. Dogs can
also be harmed with heavy exposure.

CLEANING PRODUCTS

Bleach, disinfectants, and detergents
are corrosive. Licking spills can burn
the mouth and throat.

BATTERIES & SILICA GEL PACKETS

Batteries can burn the mouth and
stomach if chewed. Silica gel packets
from packaging are a choking risk
and can upset the stomach.

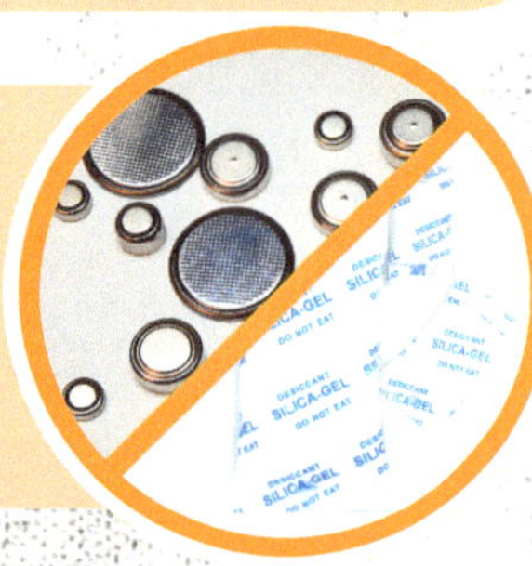

ANTIFREEZE (ETHYLENE GLYCOL)

Even small amounts can cause acute
kidney failure. Sweet taste attracts
pets. Keep away from garages and
driveways.

**Store cleaners and chemicals
out of paw's reach.**

HOUSEHOLD
PART 2
Everyday cleaners and chemicals
that irritate or poison.

MOTHBALLS

Mothballs release toxic fumes and are dangerous if chewed. Exposure may cause vomiting, anemia & weakness. Keep sealed and away from pets.

DRYER SHEETS

Fabric softeners contain irritating surfactants. Chewing can cause drooling, mouth burns, and GI upset. Keep all sheets out of reach.

HOT/COLD PACKS

Some packs contain ethylene glycol or ammonium salts. Leaks can lead to vomiting and serious illness. Discard damaged packs & block pet access.

PAINTS & SOLVENTS

Thinners and solvents can burn skin and lungs. Swallowing hydrocarbons risks aspiration pneumonia. Ventilate well and keep containers closed.

Secure storage prevents emergencies.

HOUSEHOLD
PART 3

Additional household items that can make pets sick.

LAUNDRY PODS & DETERGENTS

Laundry Pods are highly caustic when punctured. Foaming vomit and mouth burns are common. Store pods high and dry.

AIR FRESHENERS & PLUG-INS

Fragrance oils can irritate airways, especially in cats. Licking residues may upset the stomach. Ventilate rooms and restrict access.

NAIL POLISH REMOVER

Acetone solvent fumes and ingestion can sicken pets. Signs include vomiting and lethargy. Cap tightly and wipe spills fast.

SALT LAMPS (HIMALAYAN)

Licking can cause dangerous sodium overdose. Signs include vomiting, tremors, and thirst. Keep lamps out of reach.

Keep lids closed and paws away.

PEST CONTROL

PART 1

Poisons and baits commonly
used in backyards.

SNAIL & SLUG BAITS

Pellets are tempting to dogs and often
eaten in gardens. Ingestion can cause
seizures and be life-threatening.

RAT BAITS

Contain anticoagulants, bromethalin,
or D3. Pets can develop internal
bleeding or collapse. Effects may
appear days after ingestion.

MOLE & GOPHER BAITS

Baits used for lawn pests can be
highly toxic. Ingestion may cause
vomiting, tremors, and seizures. Keep
pets away from treated areas.

FERTILIZERS & COMPOST

Some products and moldy scraps
contain toxins. Ingestion can cause
vomiting, tremors, or seizures.

**Backyard baits can be deadly.
Supervise pets outdoors.**

ANT BAITS & GELS

Flavorings attract curious pets. Ingestion can cause vomiting and diarrhea. Place baits where pets cannot reach.

INSECTICIDES

Pyrethroids and organophosphates can harm pets. Signs include tremors, drooling, and seizures. Keep products off fur and away from paws.

TERMITE & CONCENTRATES

Concentrated formulas are much stronger. Small exposures can cause severe poisoning. Store locked and mix outdoors only.

HERBICIDES (WEED KILLERS)

Freshly treated lawns can irritate skin and gut. Licking paws may cause drooling and vomiting. Keep pets off treated areas until fully dry.

Keep pets off treated areas until fully dry.

PEST CONTROL

PART 3

Concentrates and granules
with higher risk.

BUG BOMBS/FOGGERS

Aerosols can irritate eyes, skin, and lungs. Licking residues may cause drooling and vomiting. Remove pets and bowls before use.

FLEA & TICK COLLARS/POWDERS

Older Carbamates and OPs can cause drooling and tremors, especially in cats. Reactions may appear within hours. Use vet-approved products only.

BORIC ACID & SILICA DUSTS

Roach and ant dusts can irritate mouths and airways. Ingestion causes drooling and stomach upset. Apply in cracks only and keep off paws.

LAWN GRUB & BEETLE KILLERS

Carbaryl or imidacloprid products may sicken pets. Eating granules can cause vomiting and weakness. Water in and keep pets off until dry.

Remove pets during use and follow label directions.

TOADS

Dogs that lick or bite toads absorb deadly toxins. This can cause frothing, seizures, or collapse. Seek urgent vet care.

HARMFUL ALGAL BLOOMS (HABS)

Blooms in ponds, lakes, and rivers. Drinking contaminated water can be rapidly fatal.

WILD MUSHROOMS

Many species contain unpredictable toxins. Treat all mushroom ingestion as an emergency.

FISHING HOOKS & LINE

Common at beaches and piers. Swallowed hooks or tangled line can cause severe internal injuries.

 **Keep adventures safe. Know the risks before you go.**

FOXTAIL GRASSES (AWNS)
Barbed seeds can burrow into ears and paws. Pets may shake, lick, or limp in pain. Avoid heavy seed areas and check after walks.

SEAWATER INGESTION
Drinking salty seawater is dangerous. It can trigger vomiting, diarrhea, and dehydration. Offer fresh water and limit beach gulping.

BEE & WASP STINGS
Stings are painful & can swell quickly. Multiple stings may be serious. Seek urgent care if breathing is affected.

JELLYFISH ON BEACHES
Beached tentacles can still sting. Contact may cause redness and pain. Rinse with seawater and call your vet.

 **Rinse paws and carry fresh water.**

ROAD SALT & DE-ICERS

Road salt used for de-icing irritates paws and can poison if licked. Signs include drooling and vomiting. Rinse paws after winter walks.

STAGNANT BUCKETS & TROUGHS

Bacteria and algae flourish in warm water. Drinking can cause vomiting and diarrhea. Empty and scrub containers often.

BAITED PUBLIC AREAS

Parks and trails may use baits. Curious pets can ingest pellets or gels. Leash up and avoid posted zones.

DISCARDED FOOD & FISH SCRAPS

Spoiled scraps grow toxins and bones injure. Scavenging can cause vomiting and blockages. Teach a strong "leave it."

Leash up and supervise closely.

emergency PET POISON REFERENCE

Quick list of the most common toxins found in homes and outdoors.

⊘ NEVER

- **Chocolate & Cocoa**
  toxic to heart and nerves
- **Grapes & Raisins**
  kidney failure in dogs
- **Onion & Garlic**
  damages red blood cells
- **Xylitol (artificial sweetener)**
  deadly to dogs
- **Macadamia Nuts**
  weakness/tremors in dogs
- **Lilies**
  toxic to cats; often fatal
- **Snail & Slug Baits**
  seizures, life-threatening
- **Rat Baits**
  can cause internal bleeding
- **Mole & Gopher Baits**
  highly toxic; some lack antidote
- **Toads**
  rapid poisoning in dogs
- **Harmful Algal Blooms**
  deadly water toxins
- **Wild Mushrooms**
  unpredictable; very toxic
- **Batteries**
  burns & heavy-metal poisoning
- **Antifreeze (Ethylene Glycol)**
  rapid kidney failure

⚠ CAUTION

- **Fatty Scraps & Cooked Bones**
  pancreatitis, gut injury, blockages
- **Fertilizers & Compost**
  mold/toxins → vomiting/tremors
- **Cleaning Products**
  corrosive; burns mouth/stomach
- **Silica Gel Packets**
  choking; GI upset if swallowed
- **Dryer Sheets**
  mouth burns, drooling & GI upset
- **Mothballs**
  vomiting, anemia, weakness
- **Insecticides/Herbicides**
  keep off treated areas until dry
- **Salt & Brines**
  high sodium → vomiting, seizures
- **Cold/Heat Packs (leaking gel)**
  leaks contain toxins; vomiting/illness
- **Cocoa Shell Mulch**
  theobromine can sicken dogs

✋ PREVENTION

- **Check labels for toxins** (xylitol, meds, chemicals)
- **Store baits and cleaners securely**
- **Keep pets off treated lawns until fully dry**
- **Leash in baited areas; supervise outdoors**
- **Rinse paws after de-icers; carry fresh water**
- **Call your vet immediately if exposure is suspected**